Living & Active

"A Faith that Moves Mountains & Fulfills Dreams"

By: Starsha Sewell, M.Ed.

Meet the Author

Starsha Sewell, M.Ed., is the CEO of Org Kulture, A training and organizational development and intellectual property think tank that provides customized solutions to complex problems. Sewell's scholarly acumen derives from her professional track record in the field of Higher Education. She has served as a University Professor, where she's taught courses in English, Business, and Economics.

At the tender age of 27 years old, she was the first African American Corporate Academic Dean at Strayer University, for its Global Region, and is a Subject Matter Expert in Education, Training, Leadership, Organizational Development, and Adult Learning. Ms. Sewell is equipped with the necessary skills to adequately facilitate, train, and release others into their fields with confidence and adequate preparation.

Sewell prides herself in her Quality Assurance capabilities, and is graced with the ability to incorporate her scholastic, professional and divine wisdom into products that aid in the faith based life skill development of individuals who desires more from the Spirit of the Living God.

CreateSpace

Printed by CreateSpace, An Amazon.com Company

Available from Amazon.com and other retail outlets

Available from Amazon.com and other online stores

Available from Amazon.com and other book stores

Available from Amazon.com, Cr eateSpace.com, and other retail outlets

A reference to an Amazon review

Available on Kindle and other devices

Available on Kindle and other retail outlets

Available on Kindle and other book stores

Available on Kindle and online stores

Table of Contents

Activate

The Word of God is living and active, and it is time to become living and active utilizing the Word of God. Are you tired of being knocked around, overlooked, and mistreated? When the strong winds of life blow in your direction, are you able to stand against the wiles of the devil; or do you find yourself falling apart at the onset of any obstacle that comes your way? What teachings are you permitting to guide your daily decisions (parental/academic /familial/communal and or religious)? Are you making sporadic choices on a daily basis or are you actively engaging in deep thought about your actions and attitudes towards your life goals? Out of all of the lists of potential influences on your life; how many independent decisions are you making without the influence of others?

Are you brining anything to the table of your own life (think about it)? The Holy Bible has laid a profound foundation for Christians, and publishers have produced some amazing translations of the Holy Bible to assist readers with its content. The Holy Bible makes it clear that Jesus prepared a table for you in the presence of your enemies. Today! Is the perfect time to decorate your table with Godly decisions.

Jesus did not place any limitations on your acquisition of the abundant life. In fact, the Word of God declares that the thief comes only to steal, kill, and destroy. While the Bible outlines the thief's mission, it obvious that the thief has no "Purpose". In fact, because you are alive today, reading this text, your actions are a direct indication that the "thief" is also a failure; who lacks the ability to hinder God's purpose for your life.

What gifts, skills, and talents have you permitted the thief to steal from you? What are you prepared to do to recover? Have you worked for many years, and now find yourself unable to do the things that you once desired? Have you studied and become certified in an area, and now your certifications are losing value, because your field is not in demand? Are you a talented athlete who was not selected for a professional league, and are now seeking a new direction? Were you a musician who did not get assigned to a major record label, and lack the resources to start your own? Were you a model, who lost the contract or the looks after rearing a child, or due to health issues? Who are you now? What are you doing with yourself? Are you satisfied, with what you are doing? What are you willing to do to change your situation? Prepare yourself and make it happen.

Discover

The Bible declares that Faith without works is dead (read: James 2:26). How many dead end situations are you permitting to remain in your life, because you are not working by faith to end those storms? What has declined your motivation for fighting the good fight of faith? And why have you become weary in your well doing? The Christian faith was built on endurance. In fact, endurance is a divine principle that guarantees the winning of the race. The word of God, never said that you have to do anything other than endure to win the race. Faith is the source of endurance; the Lord is your strength and your shield (read: Psalm 28:7) the joy of the Lord is your strength (read: Nehemiah 8:10); and when you understand each of these things plainly it blesses you with the ability to trust in the Lord with all of your heart and to lean not on your understanding during a time of endurance. God never said that we had to understand the process during the season of endurance; He simply instructed us to take action. The Bible is a Holy doctrine that illustrates divine policies and procedures for the "living and active" lifestyle in Christ Jesus.

Reading this text, alone is moving you forward in a Godly direction. Moving forward in the direction of God, does not always indicate a smooth sail. However, the opposition is only occurring because your Heavenly answered your prayer immediately, when He heard your cry. The bible indicates that Daniel experienced delay, despite the fact that His prayer was immediately answered by God. (read: Daniel 10:12). While, the King resisted Daniel, God did not. Think about the life of Job, who was afflicted in every area of His life; He was restored by God the Father. Think about Jesus Christ (the son of God), who afflicted on the cross; He was resurrected by God the Father. The Christian Faith is a resilient faith, and is rooted in the Power of Resurrection through Jesus Christ sealed salvation.

The Bible properly depicts various obstacles and blessings that believers can anticipate during their walk of salvation in the land of the living, and demonstrates to Christians today that our faith is also rooted in the struggle of humanity with itself. Jesus was the only person who did not struggle with His humanity, and it is exclusively through Him that Christian believers have the power to overcome their sinful nature.

We often hear motivational stories that boast about the comeback of celebrities, after they have fallen for whatever cause. If celebrities have the ability to succeed, fall down, and come back; you can do the same thing as well. The primary area that Christians need to apply this notion to is in their personal relationship with God; especially when they are living in a backslidden state. There is no such thing as being so dirty in the sight of God that He is unwilling to love, forgive, and restore you into relationship with Him. Okay, so you cheated on God, with your own desires, now what? Are you going to continue to cheat on Him, or are you going to return home to and build a happy family? He is waiting on you, and has been faithful in your absence.

You are a Christian and your Spiritual DNA includes the Power of Resurrection. It's Not Optional!! You must know it and you must own it!! Throw away your renters mentality, you are a Child of the Most High God, OWN Your Identity in Jesus Christ, and do not let anything shift your atmosphere!

SELF DISCOVERY

List 3 Business Goals (Dreams) that You would like to Fulfill?

1. _____
   _____
   _____
   _____

2. _____
   _____
   _____
   _____

3. _____
   _____
   _____
   _____

S-STRENGTH W-WEAKNESSES O-OPPORTUNITIES T-THREATS

TOUGH QUESTION FOR SELF-REFLECTION

What are your Spiritual Strengths, Physical/ Emotional/& Spiritual Weaknesses, Current Opportunities & Oppositions that compete with the fulfillment of your dreams, and Threats to the Fulfilment of Your Dreams?

1. **List Your Spiritual Strengths**

2. **Identify Your Physical Weaknesses**

3. **Identify Your Emotional Weaknesses**

4. **Identify Your Spiritual Weaknesses**

5. **What are your Current Opportunities?**

6. **What Oppositions (past and present) are competing with the fulfillment of your dreams?**

7. **What Threats (past and present) are competing with the fulfillment of your dreams?**

Life Changes

Employees in the role of leadership are often faced with the responsibility of leading subordinates. However, many leaders are not formally trained to effectively lead others. In life, you are going to be tasked with responsibilities that you will not be compensated or recognized for. However, you are divinely mandate to do your best anyway, because God is watching and His rewards are greater. We are in a season, where God is watching His faithful servants and is about to release life changing blessings to bless them now. The Word of God, promises to deliver a New Heaven and a New Earth. People cannot comprehend God's vivid description so they dismiss the idea that the Lord can manifest a New Heaven and Earth, while they live. However, they also proclaim belief in the miraculous. Ironically, the world is changing right before our eyes. The weather is doing unexpected things, in fact, the weather was 70 degrees in my hometown on Christmas Day in 2015; when in fact, the normal temperature is generally 34 degrees at Christmas time.

Despite the rhetoric that will have you thinking that the world is changing; the Earth is still the Lords and the fullness thereof. The Word of God is still true, and the mere fact that people are disobeying it is not an indication that the world is changing, but does suggest that the people therein are. With this, I am going to introduce you to a concept called "emotional intelligence". If you are going to lead "Living and Active" you must increase your emotional intelligence so that you cannot be manipulated, or deterred from your divine assignment. Lack of knowledge, experience, and expertise in the field of leadership prohibits organizational leaders from leading with emotional intelligence, and God will not have you ignorant.

He does not desire for any of His children to perish from the lack of knowledge. This is the primary reason that this text incorporates the word of God into the lesson, along with research that deals with the development of your human nature. It is possible to be physically alive and spiritually dead. The Goal of eternal life is to introduce you to a life sustaining relationship with Jesus and the His Father (the one who sent Him), according to John 17:3; this relationship equips you with the ability to be alive spiritually and physically in a life of consecration that will eliminate sin and your desire to sin. Eternal life is the path to an everlasting life; while sin is the path to death.

Many organizations are moving beyond training, hiring, and retiring staff; they are building teams of entrepreneurs who will help develop and shape the vision and mission of their independent organizations. This model is best depicted on television shows like "Shark Tank", where there is a culture of assistance, but there is not a long term dependency. In this instance, the system of visioning impacts leaders and followers and focuses more on the cohesive nature of visioning (what can I do to help you become successful without becoming fully vested and without taking a loss). Great thinking is the greatest asset that any company can have, because it creates a culture of efficiency. We do not "work busy" we think before we work.

With this, you must learn to remain competitive and relevant. Even if you become the Corporate Executive Officer (CEO) of your own company, or are currently the CEO of your company; you are mandated to remain in touch with the shifting trends of organizational leadership. This will help you to retain quality staff and to keep the morale of your employees in tune with your vision so that they will remain committed to helping you fulfill it. CEO's are not at liberty to look down on their staff, especially when they do not know and understand the value that each team member bring to the table of their organization.

"Goleman's research at nearly 200 large, global companies revealed that emotional intelligence—especially at the highest levels of a company is the sine qua non for leadership. Without it, a person can have first-class training, and incisive mind, and an endless supply of good ideas, but he still won't make a great leader (Goleman, 2002 p.1)"

Vision

Vision is defined as an action item that a leader must have followers implement. What is your vision? Where do you see yourself in one, three, five and ten years from now (think about it)? Many employees fail to realize, that while they are consumed with the daily tasks and responsibilities of their positions. The companies that they work for are projecting one, three, five and ten year plans to forecast their business progressions. What are you doing to track your individual progression for your life?

"The visioning and the process of visioning helps to forge group consciousness and dedication, and it helps to clarify tasks, enabling peak perform. The vision also acquaints outsiders with the group and its endeavors in a manner likely to foster appreciation and support" (Williams, 1985 p.3).

Employees of most organizations are impacted by some form of leadership be it organized or non-established; Northouse (2004), defines leadership to be a process whereby an individual influences a group of individuals to achieve a common goal. Goleman (2002), suggests that effective leaders are those who keenly aware of the five components of Emotional Intelligence: Self-Awareness, Self- Regulation, Motivation, Empathy, and Social Skill.

Transition

Reflectively, the evolution of generation gaps are greatly impacting most seasoned professionals the decision to return to school to pursue their Degree, due to the shifting demands of the workforce. While working as a Dean, I served many students that varied in age and professional acumen. Majority of my students were first-time degree seekers, who were hoping to increase their earning potential. In today's market, a solid combination of work experience and education must spark your entrepreneurial capability. You really cannot afford to entrust your skills and creative abilities to an employer that is not a team player. However, you can trust yourself to do what's best for you, because the parent company era is slowly fading.

Technology is greatly impacting the workplace and small business, and there are some amazing small businesses that offer profound services and treat their staff well; but do not have the resources and capabilities to expand. Technology, has helped businessmen and women grow and develop home based businesses; and has assisted aging business owners with remaining marketable.

When I served as a quality assurance specialist, I was responsible for training faculty who were not members of the information age, and often times they felt threatened by the impact of technology. This same trend is observed in the courts. However, with the increasing need for accountability technology is the best venue to assist with data management, and can be learned by anyone at any age if the individual is open to learning a new skill set. In life, we must remain teachable, so that you can evolve with time and remain marketable.

Seniority does not indicate quality, it only represents chronology. – ORG KULTURE

"Evolving generation gaps could alter future adult lives and careers. One obvious gap has emerged as access to computers has made computer literacy during childhood increasingly prevalent among people born, for instance, since the mid-1980. Among earlier cohorts, computer literacy remains less prevalent. What this "digital divide" portends over the long term is uncertain. There is cause for concern that disparities in Internet access could create a society of information "haves" and "have-nots" (although the increasing access among have-nots as costs of Internet access continue to fall somewhat tempers this concern (Morrison 2001 p.3)."

While, the use of technology in the workplace impose some unique challenges and in some instances a digital divide, for staff members that are not adequately trained; technology allows us to reach consumers in remote locations who would not otherwise have access to our products and services. With this notion, it is imperative for individuals with an online presence to continuously work to identify their leadership traits and behaviors so that they may continuously work to develop their emotional intelligence. Emotional intelligence is a form of discernment that enables an individual to make a godly decision rather than a carnal in faith based environments. In business, emotional intelligence guides thought processes to ensure objective communication. Emotional intelligence alleviates hypothetical analysis and deals exclusively with facts. For example, a person that lacks emotional intelligence will assume that I am sad, if I am not smiling. In contrast, an emotional intelligent person would ask me how do I feel; and would reach their conclusion based on the facts rather than an assumption.

Connections

Connections and audience awareness are important factors that help strengthen communication. This concept is traced through Cornish works as he suggests that visions move and inspire is by stating the reasons for working collaboratively. In order, for a group of people to work together effectively, they must be informed of the appropriate processes for completing the task. How does one arrive at the appropriate process? They must communicate.

Nanus' proposes a formula for visionary leadership, which suggests that Vision + Communication = Shared Purpose; it is apparent that connections within organizations add value to the human capital and their emotional stability. Employees are more beneficial to an organization when they buy into the vision of the company, and feel motivated influenced by their work in a positive way.

Technology

The integration of technology in some essence has almost removed a sense of human nature, concern, and care from virtual forums. In fact, the virtual forums have become a database of information exchange; rather than a presence felt, sociable, resulting a social disconnect in in online business to consumer relationships. Why am I sharing this? Because, if you are going to start, grow and expand your market, you must understand the platform and yourself, because the art of managing people online is totally different from managing people that you see in person daily. Unlike, most Dean's, I was professionally responsible for managing people who I could not see. Therefore, my work responsibilities are conducive to the concept of faith.

The online world is a market that must be taken care of, and you must treat your clients just as you would like to be treated, and demand the same respect, because some of your clients will have an out of sight, out of mind mentality towards you; however, your follow- up communications, professionalism and emotional intelligence will prepare you to adequately manage the unseen. Many people think that the quality of business and service is lost online. However, my expertise and knowledge in the field allows me to know that the incorporation of technology into business is the best thing for individuals who how to work technology, and who also know how technology works.   If you are going to live an active life in business, learn technology and its behind the scenes capabilities, because they will become your best friend in every business transaction, and will protect you from fraudsters.

Accountability

Many organizations refuse to take accountability for their failures. In fact, many organizational leaders instead choose to blame or ridicule employees on lower end of the pay scale for mishaps and unfortunate occurrences. However, this type of behavior is mostly displayed in organizational leaders who lack emotional intelligence. With this, Org Kulture will instill in its readers that they must handle their staff ethically. Larsen (1996) looks at the organization as a system, and focuses how the system governs its people and their interactions with the internal and external environment. "The shared vision of an organization must be built of the individual's vision of its members (Larsen, 1996).

Employees are more beneficial to the organization when they buy into the vision of the company and feel motivated an influenced by their work in a positive way. Building and developing staff that consist of dedicated team members, organizational learners, and situational leaders would be the ideal goal of an effective organizational leader;

> "Situational leadership is a perspective approach to leadership that suggests how leaders can become effective in many different types of organizational settings involving a wide variety of organizational tasks. This approach provides a model that suggests to leaders how they should behave based on the demands of a particular situation" (Northouse 2004, pp. 106).

Northouse (2004) asserts that there are four major strengths to the situational approach; 1. Situational leadership is recognized as a standard for training employees to become leaders; 2. It is a practical approach that is simple to understand and apply; 3. The approach set forth guidelines outlining the characteristics employees

13

should implement to enhance their skills; and 4. Situational leadership emphasizes that there is not one "best" style of leadership; and conveys that leaders should remain flexible and adapt their style to the requirements of any situation. A leader who utilizes this approach, will be most effective.

Organizational leaders must have a clear vision on their organizational path and vision. The Situational leadership theoretical model suggest that being assigned leadership responsibilities do not suffice the requirement of being an effective leader, nor does it indicate the person assigned these sorts of tasks are capable of leading others. Individuals will assume additional roles and responsibilities if they believe that it will contribute to their success with a company. However, the ultimate goal of being "Living and Active" is that you proceed with assuring knowing the tangible benefits of your hard work and effort. The Living and Active life style is not a guessing game; it is an action plan.

"Path-goal theory emphasizes the relationship between the leader's style and the characteristics of the subordinates and the work setting. The underlying assumption of path-goal theory is derived from the expectancy theory, which suggests that subordinates will be motivated if they think they are capable of performing their work, if they believe their efforts will result in a certain outcome, and if they believe that the payoffs for doing their work are worthwhile (Northouse, 2004: p.123)".

__Thinking & Learning__

Goleman adds a comparative analysis of mental models and anatomy to demonstrate the semantic concepts of emotional experiences of self and of others. "The reason a leader's manner—not just what he does, but how he does it – matters so much lies in the design of the human brain: What scientist have begun to call the open-loop nature of the limbic system, our emotional centers. A closed loop system such as the circulatory system is self-regulating; what's happening in the circulatory system of others around us does not impact our own systems. An open- loop system depends largely on external sources to manage itself. In other words, we rely on connections with other people for our own emotional stability" (Goleman, 2002).

Argyris described learning as a two-prong process which involved single and double loop learning. The fact that single loop learning is like a thermostat that learns when it is too hot or too cold and turns the heat on or off. Secondly, it was Double loop learning occurs when error is detected and corrected in ways that involve the modification of an organization's underlying norms, policies and objectives (Argyris, 1978; 1982; 1990)". Considering the fact that the double loop learning approach creates energy, desire to know, and the gain of more understanding. It leads many to the concept of how to learn and lead effectively. I would be a disservice to neglect the evaluation of a leader and their emotional intelligence.

Goleman (2002) suggests that to enhance emotional intelligence, organizations must refocus their training to include the limbic system. Organizations must be willing to help people break old behavioral habits and establish new ones.

"The key is uncovering your ideal self – the person you would like to be, including what you want in your life and work. That is the "first discovery" of the self-directed learning process (Goleman, 2002: pg. 116)."

Marquandt, suggests that the evolution of a new economy will require the skill sets and contributions acquired by professionals in academic programs who are learning to become learning organizations; and for those that are building and developing organizational learners. "The need to pursue work-related learning in today's knowledge organization is among the many revolutions of the new economy. The heart, growth, innovation, and distinctiveness of learning organizations derive from the ability to utilize human capital. And the fundamental business challenge is how to attract, deploy, develop, adapt, and retain it better than anyone else (Marquandt, 2002: pg.111).

Often times, leaders are faced with the challenge of leading others, this is not an easy task; especially when you have little or no time to reflect on your own past and purpose. People who live and perform high powered jobs without knowing their purpose often times deal with others carelessly, because they are unhappy/unfulfilled.

Professionally, we must be cognitively aware of how to perceive others in the role of a subordinate, whether they work for you, or are your customer. Culturally, and for the love of money many non-faith based organizations have adopted the "Customer Is Always Right" trend. However, learning organizations must create cultures of accountability and work at best to educate their consumers, even if they do not come back again. When your organization is branded as an "emotional intelligent" organization, consumers will respect your work and value your time, service, and your learning organization.

Learning organizations are not "anything goes" organizations. Learning organizations understand the reason that they exist. – Org Kulture

Faith based learning organizations are driving forces. Everything that faith based learning organizations do must align with the vision and the mission of the organizational leaders God given purpose. Faith based learning organizations do not randomly drive from one place to another; we will arrive at our destinations safely and efficiently with every move that we make by faith in Jesus name, because we trust God's divine instructions. Every move that we make, is a part of God's strategic plan whether it's written or spoken through a prophetic word. We must walk in sync with our vision and mission, and must be willing to become transformational and transparent to ensure that the mission of God is accomplished.

The Word of God decrees that we are overcome by the blood of the Lamb and the power of our testimony. Therefore, transparency in your walk with God is a pre-requisite for the abundant life in Jesus Christ. The blood of the Lamb gives us the ability to overcome the guilt, shame, and hurt that's rooted in past sins; and it is the exposure of the impact of these things on our lives that invites our deliverance. You have to welcome your deliverance into your life, by presenting your body as a living sacrifice unto God holy and acceptable. When we sow ourselves unto God, we reap more of Him, and this alone is the greatest example of a divine transfer.

Teamwork

Team work is an essential element for success, and should not be regarded as a limitation. Providing the example of a team project, where it might be challenging to meet with group members to identify and address specific needs of the project directly. One will have to move forward with a consensus that was established by the group in order to prevent failure.

While this example, is not an effective demonstration of leaders within learning organizations; it does in fact, convey one's ability to buy into the mission and vision of a shared idea or perception. Learning organizations will make time to meet and will adhere to the demands of the group project, because emotional intelligent people are committed to their tasks; and they understand that their work reflects their individual contribution. Most people in group settings, think that "group think" conceals their personal accountability and creates anonymity. However, it does not; because when we dissect each individual role that contributes to the project or the demise of a system; the actions of each group participant can be weighed utilizing research methodology.

"A" players are generally the leaders in learning organizations, if the C-level executives are emotional intelligent and involved in their learning organization. Authentic learning organizations are wise enough to hire "A" players exclusively, because it is unwise to affiliate yourselves with, or to do business with people who do not have a learning organization mindset. Sure, they might go through the ranks and meet all of the requirements professionally. However, are immature and prideful, because they are validated by their success that was achieved through the systems of formality and was never subjected to a 360 degree feedback assessment.

360 Degree Feedback In Politics

In fact, 360 degree assessments should be mandated by the people for the people. We elect politicians with our votes, and once they are in office rarely express our satisfaction or dissatisfaction with their Public Service. Often times, we take an inactive role in legislature and fail to hold politicians accountable for things that they implement that do not represent our interests collectively. We must elect people whose life values are consistent with our moral and spiritual convictions; it is not enough to select strangers who are labeled in a demographic to represent your interest. In fact, it is a misconception to even think that these individuals are concerned about you or me; when in fact, their role is designed to give them a place in the Federal government for your State. So what you find happening here, is that the interest of your State is being advanced in the Courts State and Federally, and also advanced by law enforcement within the same system; and these attacks come after one has engaged in or has requested "constituent services".

What say are the people given, when they are failed by systems, currently there is nothing in place? 360 degree assessments would give folks a say, and ultimately constituents would be permitted to remain anonymous. I have never struggled with being honest and transparent with politicians or the courts, because we must hold accountable bad actors, wherever they exist.

Our Nation is far too young to have been subjected to all of the dysfunction that it has endured in its treatment of people for reasons that they cannot change; and since the laws on the books have progressed; why are the courts giving us so much opposition? Why are people of color and the colorless indigent being oppressed in the areas of employment, housing, and family in 2016?

I am Overcome By The Blood Of The Lamb & Power of My Testimony

Have the courts become complacent with modern day slavery? Are United States Citizens dealing with, the same people who segregated prior to the changes of the laws on the books; have they found a new way to implement the laws on the books exclusively for the "appearance" of justice? My qualitative review empirical research data that was acquired for the course of three years from litigations on the United States docket it reflects that sound judicial precedent in the Fourth Circuit has not been enforced since 1996. Furthermore, the researcher discovered that the same precedent has not even been applied to civil rights removals from 1996 to the present; although the case law was alluded to in 2006. When, I think about my procedural history within the Fourth Circuit and the housing crisis that was inflicted by the courts in the State of Maryland, it reminds me about the story of the 39th Vice President of the United States, Spiro Agnew, who according to his book and Time.com claimed his innocence regarding the bribery accusations. In fact, historical articles indicate that Diana Motz relied on the admission of his Attorney after Agnew wrote a book declaring his innocence.

Ironically, State of Maryland Judicial Trustee's entered my personal information into the State's database asserting that I sold my home to the State of Maryland Housing and Community Development Administration for $153,000 dollars on May 18, 2011; this was done by the same Trustees who filed fraudulent documents on the courts indicating that my they sold my home to Dawn Neuman for $153,000 dollars on February 12, 2010. Even with the Trustees testimony asserting that another Trustee sold the house to CDA on May 18, 2011, the Federal court still concealed the fraud of the trustee who engaged in identity theft, because the identity theft occurred under the leadership of the Federal Judges Daughter.

Ironically, Judge Diana G. Motz, who was appointed by former President William "Bill" Clinton, and who wrote the binding precedent in the United States Court of Appeals, Fourth Circuit. In re Katherine Susan LOWE, Petitioner. No. 96–560. | Argued Oct. 30, 1996. | Decided Dec. 17, 1996, certifying that remand orders in civil rights removals are reviewable; violated the law upon failing to perform her judicial responsibilities in her official capacity of Judicial Officer, because she had a vested interest in concealing fraud of her daughter. When, Motz served as an Assistant Attorney General in the Maryland Attorney General's office, and was the Chief Litigator in the 1981 case against the former governor of Maryland, Spiro Agnew.

According to Msa.Maryland.gov "Her advice to the court was to "send a message to public official and ordinary citizens everywhere that public officials are not only elected by the people but.. are answerable to the people." However, empirical research data that I collected from my filings which were used as qualitative assessments; the researcher found that Diana Motz is selective in sending messages to public officials, especially when the public official at issue is her daughter.

While, Diana Motz is a Democrat, who did not have a problem with fining Spiro Agnew, who was a Republican; she struggles with holding her Republican Husband Frederick Motz accountable for his abuse of discretion and judicial bias in the District court, in her official capacity as a Judge in the Fourth Circuit. The Researcher also discovered that Diana Motz failed to send the message that she sent to Spiro Agnew to her Daughter Catherine Motz, when she served as the Chief of Staff at the Maryland Community Housing Development Administration; and permitted the use of my personal information in connection with fraud.

The Researchers Judicial empirical research data, was required through qualitative research methodology over the course of three years shows that State officials and Federal Judicial officers who formerly served as State Prosecutors were literally working to protect their organized criminal enterprise that they built overtime through tradition identified by the Washington Post as the "**Attorneys from the Baltimore legal establishment**".

Upon analyzing, the procedural judicial actions of Judge Diana Motz it appears that she only targets "public officials elected by the people". Her procedural History on the Public Access Court Electronic Records

(PACER), reveals that she permits and willfully conceals the fraud of State of Maryland Officials, and the fraud of those who have appointed positions that do not involve the votes of the people. Judge Motz enjoys publically embarrassing and shaming individuals with her judicial misconduct. However, has literally shamed and embarrassed her entire family due to her own judicial prejudice, bias, racial prejudice, and violations of my religious freedom.

My procedural history and qualitative assessments of the State and Federal courts through the collection of qualitative empirical research data from the State of Maryland and Federal court captures the judicial bias of Judges who formerly served as Attorney Generals in the State of Maryland. Research shows that these Judges are utilizing legal strategies to advance the interest of Attorney Generals and States Attorneys who currently served in the State of Maryland. The scheme is found in case assignment; States Attorneys and Attorney Generals get their cases assigned to Judges that formerly served as a State Attorney, Attorney General position, or US Attorney for the State of Maryland, and all for the past three years have willfully and violated Federal law, and have engaged in the deprivation of rights of Maryland Citizens and are advancing the interest of the State of Maryland collectively as organized crime. These Judges are willfully violating precedent, and selectively issue non-binding orders for the people that they choose to oppress.

Their abuse of judicial systems is not sporadic in fact it is has been adopted as a strategic practice in violation of the Fourth Circuit Policy and the rule of law that requires cases to be decided on the merits. However, cases are being assigned and prematurely dismissed based on who the action is against and Judges are engaging in impeachable offences. According to Time.com, "Agnew is widely considered by historians to be among the worst Vice Presidents in the history of the United States." Agnew is not the worst, because he deserves to be. Agnew was an elected official who was targeted, because he refused to be silenced by the Maryland Attorney Generals.

The facts in this writing, were acquired through research qualitative research methodology that was acquired from the State Courts and Federal Judicial system for over a course of five years. The qualitative judicial researcher and qualitative judicial assessments were plain and positioned for the appearance of a claim.

The researcher began this study after, she first litigated in the Federal Courts in Missouri, and discovered a causal connection between her experiences in Missouri to the experience that she had in Maryland. She noticed that the local rules in the Missouri courts were rigged to assist the Appellee's. This matter was addressed to the Supreme Court and on judicial complaint, but there is not a culture of accountability in the Eight Circuit.

The Researcher filed claims using the content of the claim were used with the sole intent to weigh how the courts treat "**facts**" and "**rules**" and the "**law**", all of the researchers claims were factual and were supported by direct evidence. However, because the Plaintiff was Pro Se; the courts disregarded the facts, rules, and the law in every single action. The research findings indicated that judicial officers are intentionally engaging in fraud on the court; and are engaging in discriminative patterns and practices when dealing with minorities and the colorless indigent. The Researcher also found that the "facts" and "local and Federal Civil rules" and the rule of "law" did not matter to the Judges in any of the litigations. These Judges were exuding an organizational culture of judicial organized crime and are advance political interest for the sources who nominated and cr appointed them to the judicial bench.

State of Maryland Housing Crisis & The Motz' Judicial Bias toward African Americans in Maryland

City's Wells Fargo lawsuit dismissed

U.S. judge calls claims of millions in predatory lending damages 'not plausible'
January 07, 2010|By Tricia Bishop | tricia.bishop@baltsun.com

A federal court judge on Wednesday dismissed Baltimore's landmark lawsuit against Wells Fargo & Co., saying it was "not plausible" that the mortgage giant triggered millions of dollars in damages, as the city claimed, by causing increased foreclosures through racist, predatory lending.
"The alleged connection is even more implausible when considered against the background of other factors leading to the deterioration of the inner city,"
 U.S. District Judge J. Frederick Motz explained in a six-page memorandum opinion accompanying the dismissal order. He pointed specifically to Baltimore's "extensive unemployment, lack of educational opportunity and choice, irresponsible parenting, disrespect for the law, widespread drug use, and violence."

Motz, who's served a long career in the city, did leave the door open for Baltimore to file a more limited complaint by Feb. 3. The city could restrict its claims to specific damages allegedly suffered because of actual houses made vacant by Wells Fargo's lending practices, he wrote.

"He's asking the city to paint with a less broad brush if it wishes to do that," City Solicitor George Nilson summarized. Counselors plan to discuss their options, which include appealing or filing a narrowed lawsuit, as early as today, he said.

Motz hinted at a hearing last month that he could dismiss the suit as too broad. The decision was in line with others across the country dismissing similar suits that were filed, like Baltimore's, in the wake of the subprime mortgage crisis.

Comparable cases, seeking compensation for alleged foreclosure losses, in Cleveland and in Birmingham, Ala., were also dismissed in their districts.

Motz's dismissal essentially said Baltimore did not have the proper "standing" - basically the right - to sue because it didn't effectively show a causal connection for its wide-ranging claims, which alleged "tens of millions" of dollars in losses.

'Reverse redlining'

Baltimore's lawsuit was said to be the first of its kind when it was filed in January 2008. It, like others, claimed Wells Fargo targeted minority borrowers for bad loans - an illegal practice known as "reverse redlining" - which allegedly led to defaults and a disproportionately high rate of foreclosures and vacancies in black or Latino neighborhoods.

Wells Fargo vehemently denies the allegations and has accused the city of being so cash-poor that it has to sue for revenue.

But city attorneys proffered affidavits of former Wells Fargo employees as evidence. And they promised to quantify the exact damages incurred. Through arguments, they claimed the reverse redlining was real and that it caused millions in losses through:

•More abandoned homes.
•Lower property values and tax revenue.
•A rise in criminal activity and law enforcement expenditures.
•An increase in social services fees and construction rehabilitation costs.

But the judge was skeptical of the scope of the city's claims. Baltimore has as many as 30,000 vacant homes, according to the original complaint, but so far, the city has identified only 80 vacancies related to Wells Fargo in African-American neighborhoods.

"Thus, using the City's own figures," Motz wrote, "Wells Fargo is responsible for only a negligible portion of the City's vacant housing stock."

Nilson said those numbers were preliminary, reflecting only a "very limited exchange of information," and he expressed disappointment in the judge's decision to dismiss before "meaningful discovery" - or evidence-gathering - could take place.

"I don't agree with all of the significant elements of the judge's analysis. But of course, he's the judge, and he wears black robes," Nilson said. "I respect his analysis even if I may not agree with it."

Wells Fargo has said there are too many possible factors to show what caused a vacancy, including the economy, unemployment or divorce.

Cara Heiden, co-president of Wells Fargo Home Mortgage, said she was pleased by the court's decision to reject the claim.

More lawsuits filed

"From the beginning, we have consistently maintained that Baltimore's economic problems could not be attributed to the negligible number of foreclosures Wells Fargo has done in Baltimore," she said.

Judge Motz's decision appears consistent with that belief, Heiden added, as do the decisions in Birmingham and Cleveland.

Still, the lawsuits keep coming. The state of Illinois filed a comparable case in July, and Memphis, Tenn., filed a suit last week.

Heiden suggested that cities were suing because of the challenging economic times, but added that the company will "vigorously defend" itself against the allegations.

"We know how it is that we go about business and doing right by the customer," she said.

Lawsuit chronology:

Jan. 8, 2008 The city sues Wells Fargo

March 21, 2008 Wells Fargo files a motion to dismiss, challenging the city's right - or "standing" - to sue

June 1, 2009 The city files an amended complaint that's more than 800 pages long with exhibits

July 2, 2009 U.S. District Judge Bensen Legg denies the motion to dismiss the suit and allows discovery to go forward

Aug. 6, 2009 The case is reassigned to Judge J. Frederick Motz

Sept. 18, 2009 Wells Fargo files a new motion to dismiss

Dec. 14, 2009 A hearing on the motion to dismiss is held

Jan. 6, 2010 Judge Motz dismisses the city's suit

http://articles.baltimoresun.com/2010-01-07/news/bal-md.wellsfargo07jan07_1_predatory-lending-dismissed-motz

The Circle: Motz Chuang Motz

Ironically, Judge J.F. Motz has a procedural history of taking over cases and reassigning them, the researcher discovered this practice in the abovementioned article; and also experienced this first hand in an action that he to date has not recused himself from. Judge J. F. Motz transferred the researcher's case to Judge Chuang, but Judge Motz did not recuse himself. Ironically, Baltimore City should petition the FBI for a Federal investigation into the actions of Judge J. F. Motz to determine if Judge J. F. Motz had standing to dismiss their case considering the fact that Judge Benson Everett Legg served as Chief Judge from January 6, 2003 to January 4, 2010; and assumed senior status on June 8, 2012, and ultimately retired from the US District Court for the District of Maryland on February 6, 2013. The researcher questioned Judge Motz' case reassignment to the Fourth Circuit, prior to discovering that Judge J. F. Motz has a habitual discriminative pattern and practice of reassigning cases in actions with the sole intent to advance the interest of Banks and Employers, at the expense of minorities and the colorless indigent.

I appreciate the Baltimore Sun's article, because it validates my theory of judicial corruption of the husband and wife judicial team Diana and J. Frederick Motz; because Judge Motz, reassigned my case to Judge Theodore Chuang and failed to recuse himself, and when I appealed the case to the Fourth Circuit his wife Diana Motz affirmed Judge Theodore Chuang judicial corruption. Judge Theodore Chuang received an exchange from the States University, for the favor that He extended the Motz, upon dismissing my case. However, it backfired; because Judge Theodore Chuang entered a decision on a case that he lacked jurisdiction to hear, because Judge Motz is still proceeding on the action for failure to recuse himself. Ironically, Senator Grassley raised concerns about Judge Theodore Chuang who provided legal counsel to the State Department and Department of Homeland Security, prior to being assigned to the Federal Bench.

According to the Hill, Senator Chuck Grassley stated [sic] ""I can't support his nomination because of the central role Mr. Chuang played in the administration's efforts to stonewall an investigation into the situation in Benghazi," Grassley said. "These questions remain unanswered because the administration refuses to recognize the rights of congressional oversight."

According to the Hill, Sen. Barbara Mikulski (D-Md.) defended Chuang, saying he was only doing his job and Grassley's "beef" was really with former Secretary of State Hillary Clinton. "I'm kind of tired of this Benghazi witch hunt stuff," Mikulski said. "He did not have decision making authority as to whether to provide documents to the committee. That decision came from higher up."

Ironically, Judge Theodore Chuang did not have decision making authority to dismiss the Researchers case due Judge J. F. Motz's failure to recuse himself. However, that did not stop Judge Chuang from stonewalling and obstructing justice in the researcher's complaint against her former employer.

The researchers are all caught scheming and concealing collectively and are preying on the weak due to financial indigence; when in fact the Maryland Middle class was made indigent, by judicial bad actors. The same judicial officers who deprived individuals of their rights to their property are the same individuals who discriminated most middle class employment litigations. Judge Chuang and J. F. Motz and Diana Motz are key examples of judicial oppressors, who have attacked middle class Americans for their property.

Leadership

Great leaders must be willing to share purpose with others, and must also be willing to define purposes clearly and also convey its significance to other organizational leaders. When team members fail to provide adequate input to a team project, you must develop a "strong finish" mindset that is required in order to complete the task with superior quality. Leaders must work extra hours when required to ensure their success in the workplace. Doing so will position you to become a profound entrepreneur, because you will acquire the emotional intelligence that is necessary to manage a learning organization and projects independently. Unfortunately, we live in a culture that works at best to create systems dependency; with this regard many people live relaxed lives within the system, and typically fail when adversity and or crisis is inflicted.

Meltdown

During the 2008, meltdown of our economy any objective observer with common sense and intellectual know that many banks prevailed and many people suffered losses and have not recovered to date. We also know that the American economy still reflects costs associated with the crisis, and that many conversations have ended about the issue. However, the issue is still affecting the American people; therefore, the conversation must continue. Learning organizations are those that masters the skill of adaptability to change. However, we also have the power to change things as well and keen ability to fix broken systems.

Learning organizations are people and are also companies. However, I would like for you to regard yourself as a learning organization. You must adapt the learning organization mindset so that you will remain adaptable and responsive to whatever comes your way. Most systems only attack individuals who appear worthless, such as the poor, needy, vulnerable, elderly, prisoners and children. However, that is the same population of people that God is specifically concerned about.

When you are on the mind of God, you are in the best position to be blessed. Sure, you have been systematically trained to rely on systems, and systems post-crisis have become more conducive to promoting ongoing hardships and failure of vulnerable populations, because there power and superiority is rooted in control. How strong are you without crisis? How weak are you with crisis? Who do you need, when you are in a crisis? Who must take care of you, when you are in a crisis? For the unbeliever, this could be governmental systems. For Christians, it's Jesus Christ. We are now living in a time when the courts are reducing and extending rights, not in the scope of limiting government, but within the scope of expanding it powers, subtly. For years, the courts have discriminatively created and applied precedent that sides with banks and insurance companies, and they are applying these precedents when addressing the litigations of people who are seeking justice.

We often times hear, that money rules the world, but my independent research has showed that judicial monetary policy actually rules the courts. If you are going to be a living and active person, you must know this because the very moment that you step into the market independently to pursue the American dream, you will have to learn the ruling precedent of the courts in order to successfully succeed at business. If we do not combat the governmental and judicial manipulation of systems, business owners and their mom and pop stores will not be driven out by monopolies, but instead will be driven out by the courts and big government.

Power Sharing

When comparing the experience of attending undergraduate school, immediately following high school, with attending graduate school as an experienced professional and adult learner in a self-directed learning environment; I discovered that there are many communication barriers associated with power sharing in distant and self-directed learning environments. When mentioning the term self-directed learning, I want you to consider the role of the individual who is learning (you or me), and their relationship with the individual who is responsible for supervising their instruction (Professor or Employer). This relationship is similar to one of a manager and employee, which indicates that some sort of power structure is involved. "Signs of power in an organization include decision-making ability and the authority to distribute rewards (such as pay raises) and punishments (such as firing people) (Ohair, Friedrich, and Dixon, 2005)".

In distant and self-directed learning environments teachers or professors have the authority to distribute rewards (in the format of a wonderful grade, resulting in passing) and punishments (in the form of a horrible grade, resulting in failure). With this, it is crucial to review four ways that power is distributed: "(1) managers [teachers or professors] hold all the power, and the worker [student] hold none; (2) neither supervisors [teachers or professors] nor workers [students] have much power; (3) workers [students] hold most of the power, and supervisors [teachers or professors] hold little; and (4) managers [teachers or professors] and workers [students] share power (Kouzes and Posner, 1987,); (Ohair, Friedrich, and Dixon, 2005)".

In a classroom setting teachers have more direct authority of the actions and interactions of their students, but in self-directed learning environments there is a struggle for control between the adult learner for independence, and the instructor for authority. "Self-direction in learning is not a set of techniques that can be applied within a context of objectives and evaluative criteria that are determined by others. At the heart of self-directedness is the adult's assumption of control over setting educational goals and generating personally meaningful evaluative criteria. One cannot be a fully self-directed learner if one is applying techniques of independent study within a context of goals and evaluative criteria determined by an external authority" (Brookfield, 1986).

According to Kouzes and Posner's explanation of the distribution of power in leadership, the fourth style is the most effective method to, utilize for alleviating communication barriers between adult learners and the instructors; because emphasizes the importance of power-sharing. Self-directed learners need facilitation and direction to remain in the context of the course. However, do not need instructors to work against their perspectives. The relationship between the adult learner and the facilitator should foster an environment of information sharing, and should not be directive. The directive approach could create conflict amongst the perspective of both parties, resulting in the failure of effective communication.

While completing 80 percent of my doctoral degree at Nova Southeastern University in Miami, Florida, I conducted a study to examine, the distribution power in distant and self-directed learning environments. I explored the communications barriers (such as conflict and tensions) that arise from power sharing, perception, perspective of the adult teacher and learner. The purpose of this study was to learn and understand various dimensions of online communications. While studying, I did not know that I would become an online Professor. However, I was blessed with the opportunity to serve online and brick and mortar students and through experiential exploration was able to master and hone skills that fosters memorable online experiences. Just because you are far apart does not mean that your connections cannot be meaningful. In fact, this is the exact concept that faith does for dreams. Just, because you cannot see your dream, does not mean that you cannot work to make it come true. Faith is all about taking action, and trusting God as your source. We make God happy when we step out on faith, because it conveys our trust. In fact, the Holy Bible declares that without faith it is impossible to please God (Hebrews 11:6).

When conducting research, I wanted to discover if self-directed learning intimidated or challenged teachers, professors, and adult learners to think outside of themselves for the sake of teambuilding. Professor do not have direct control over the actions of students in online environments and do not have any eye contact in asynchronous environments. Hence, online Professors are the forerunners in adapting to the diverse utilization of authority, perspective, perception, and power with the use of technology. Hence, they must be self-controlled and emotionally intelligent.

I also explored if the intimidation of self-directed learning affect professors' and adult learner's perception of one another; and if their contrasting views created conflict; Online Professors must have discernment to an extent, because students are not always trained or equipped with necessary skills to utilize online educational platforms; while Professors on the other hand are provided with training as an employment requisite.

In order to adequately determine if adult learners and instructors have the ability to work collaboratively with respect to one another's distribution of power or a tone of guidance must be established by the Professor, so that Students will not feel alone in the online world. While there courses are self-directed, the instruction is Professor directed; and Professors must remain leaders of a student population that they cannot physically see.

Many academic professionals arrive to the teaching profession, ducking and dodging the perspectives of their educators in efforts to maintain their own since of originality. However, when arriving to the teaching profession, they impose their perspectives on individual's that have their own set of valid values and beliefs. Should conflict arise, when everyone is entitled to focus and establish their individual interests? Or should the individual compromise their perspective or share of power to meet the needs of the other? Working adults, who participate voluntarily in higher academia face similar challenges in efforts to retain their values and beliefs; they duck and dodge perspectives of their educators in efforts to maintain their own since of originality.

When, adults participate in higher academia, it does not necessarily indicate that they are lacking skill. Each individual has to decide their own purpose for their pursuits of higher academia. However, in a distant learning environment the challenge of understanding the perspective of both parties become greater, because the face-to face communication is absent. In self-directed settings professors are faced with the challenge of reviewing and learning the perspective of a student of whom they have never seen face to face; and therefore, are challenged to judge the student based solely on their presentation of work, perspective, and tone. This notion holds truth for the student as well, because self-directed professors assume that their students' thoroughly understand their perspectives. However, make this assumption without consideration to the fact that information is process differently. When students make efforts to rectify errors and misunderstandings; Instructors of self-directed learners should work with their students to foster an effective learning environment.

The spectrum associated with facilitating adult learning is challenging for teachers and professors alone, because there is very little resources that focuses thoroughly on adult education. Houle's work of 1988, made the following observation: "When some people began to think that it might be interesting or significant to deal directly with the learning desires or processes of the individual, the idea was greeted with apathy or scorn, particularly so far as self-directed learning was concerned". This view notes that some educators were against the potential threats that self-directed learning could impose. With this, it is almost apparent to understand the reason why adult learning and its importance has been given little consideration by educators and researchers. The idea alone imposes a threat to the need and utilization of the educator's professional industry.

"Therefore, studying learning within the natural environment of adults' everyday life had not been considered worthwhile or even possible. Tied in with this perspective is the role of educators of adults. Should we be working with learners outside the formal institutional environment? And might we be cutting into our own "business" as educators if we acknowledge that many adults can learn very effectively without our assistance? Despite these concerns, the study of self-directed learning has emerged as one [of] the major thrusts of adult education research over the past three decades (Merriam and Caffarella, 1999)".

Authentic Educators are not concerned about the "Business of Education", but are concerned about the Students'. Facilitation is the best way to foster and develop independent thinkers, and I am happy that the industry continues to evolve self-directed forums. While, self-directed learning will never remove the need of facilitators and subject matter experts; it has merely shifted the role of facilitator from "Educator" to "Educational Leader". Educators who are not effective leaders, will struggle with managing students in on online learning environment; because Self- Directed learners do not need to be instructed they need to be navigated and professionally trained to create solutions.

Released Destiny

Reflect on your responses to the assessments on pages 1 through 8. These areas have prohibited you from acquiring and fulfing your dreams. Now that you have exposed your personal obstables, do not permit them to delay you from pursuing your dreams. You can do all things through Christ Jesus who stregthens you! The Word of God is Living and Active in your life, now! Trust God by Faith and start Working on your Dreams!

Works Cited:

"America's Worst Vice Presidents Spiro Agnew". Time.com. August 21, 2008. Retrieved January 18, 2016.

Argyris, C., & Schön, D. (Argyris,1978; 1982;1990) *Organizational learning: A theory of action perspective,* Reading, MA: Addison Wesley.

Brookfield, Stephen D., Understanding and Facilitating Adult Learning John Wiley& Sons, Inc. Copyright 1986.

Bishop, Tricia,"City's Wells Fargo lawsuit dismissed". http://articles.baltimoresun.com/2010-01-07/news/bal-md.wellsfargo07jan07_1_predatory-lending-dismissed-motz. January 07, 2010. Retrieved January 18. 2016

Cornish, E. (2004). Futuring: The exploration of the future. Bethesda, MD: World Future Society.

Datamonitor SWOT Analysis, from Business Source Premier Database
Datamonitor. (2009, May 8). McCormich & Company, Inc. SWOT analysis. Retrieved June 2, 2010, from Business Source Complete database.

Goleman, D., Boyatzis, R., & McKee, A. (2002). *Primal leadership.* Boston:

Harvard Business School Press. ISBN 157851486X.

J. Kouzs and B.Z. Posner, The Leadership Challenge (San Francisco: Jossey-Bass, 1987).

Larsen, K., McInerney, C., Nyquist, C., Santos, A., & Silsbee, D. (1996). *Learning Organizations*. Retrieved from http://home.nycap.rr.com/klarsen/learnorg January 29, 2007.

Marquandt, M.J. (2002) *Building learning organization* (2nd ed.) Palo Alto, CA: Davies & Black Publishing.

Merriam, Sharan B. and Caffarella, Rosemary S. Learning in Adulthood: A Comprehensive Guide. 2nd edition. Jossey-Bass A Wiley Imprint., 1999

Morrison, P. A. (2001). A demographic perspective on our nation's future. Washington, DC:

RAND Publications.

Nanus, B. & Dobbs, S. (1999) *Leaders Who Make A Difference: Essential Strategies for Meeting the Nonprofit Challenge.* San Francisco, CA: Jossey-Bass Publishers.

Northouse, P. G. (2004). Leadership theory and practice (3rd ed.) Thousand Oaks, CA: Sage Publications Inc.

O'Hair, Dan, G. W. Friedrich, and L. D. Shaver. Strategic Communication in Business and the Professions. 4th edition. Houghton Mifflin Co., 2002.

Saperstein, Saundra. Tradition Influences Job of Md. Attorney. https://www.washingtonpost.com/archive/local/1981/06/25/tradition-influences-job-of-md-attorney/d1698cb0-a0a2-4aaf-9c93-9b45bd76d4d3/. June 25, 1981. Retrieved January 19, 2016

www.ingramcontent.com/pod-product-compliance
Lightning Source LLC
Chambersburg PA
CBHW081543280526
45788CB00010B/3347